I0016660

Get I.T.!

How to Start a Career in the New Information Technology

How to Start as a Data Scientist

By Murat Aytekin, Zorina Alliata

With many thanks to Monika Megyesi

Copyright © 2016

Publisher: Better Karma Publishing

www.BetterKarmaPublishing.com

All rights reserved. No part of this book may be reproduced or transmitted in any form or by any means without written permission from the author.

ISBN 978-0-9962897-5-7

TABLE OF CONTENTS

1. IS THIS JOB A GOOD FIT FOR YOU?

A Data Scientist looks at a lot of data from various sources, finds interesting patterns and insights, and predicts which ones will add value.

Thinking like a Data Scientist

Did your Mom use to scold you all the time for being too nosy? Did you get into trouble for picking all your toys apart in tiny pieces to see how they really work? Did random people lecture you about how curiosity killed the cat?

Have you tried playing the stock market and predict if a stock went up or down, based on its history, or news, or recent events? Are you a big fan of the March Madness brackets and calculating possible winners?

Then you might have some qualities that can help you become a data scientist.

Data Science is not an easy area to get into, but it is not impossible. I know personally several people who have done it, coming from diverse and unrelated backgrounds.

You have to have a head for numbers, curiosity, and sheer passion for a science that can predict the future.

2. WHAT IS THE JOB?

A Data Scientist is really a scientist. They apply rigorous scientific principles to analyzing data. If there weren't any computers invented, the Data Scientists would have done their work by hand, using a lot of math. But because they now use computers and many helpful software tools in their work, they have become a part of the Information Technology working force.

Let's first define some of the terms we use in this book.

What is Data?

Data are facts. Data can be a measurement (e.g. temperature, height, game scores), a record (you're your address, name) or an observation (e.g. your mood, gender, education). Think of it as tiny containers holding one piece of information. By itself, each piece might not mean anything; however, in the right context, the pieces together can paint a very complete image of you and your likely qualities.

There is a LOT of data in the world, and everyone is rushing to produce even more. As of 2016, more data has been produced in the previous two years than it has ever been in the history of the world. Think of a Byte as a small enough container to contain only one letter or number. Then look at the sizes of data we work with in today's world:

Name	Size	Size in Bytes
Bit	1 bit	1/8
Byte	8 bits	1
Kilobyte	1,024 bytes	1,024
Megabyte	1,024 kilobytes	1,048,576
Gigabyte	1,024 megabytes	1,073,741,824
Terrabyte	1,024 gigabytes	1,099,511,627,776
Petabyte	1,024 terrabytes	1,125,899,906,842,624
Exabyte	1,024 petabytes	1,152,921,504,606,846,976
Zettabyte	1,024 exabytes	1,180,591,620,717,411,303,424
Yottabyte	1,024 zettabytes	1,208,925,819,614,629,174,706,176

Many Data Scientists work in the Big Data industry - where huge quantities of data are available and need to be analyzed and aggregated.

Data Analysis is the process of applying statistical and/or logical techniques to describe, visualize, and evaluate data. Data Scientists will use data analysis a lot during the data exploration phase.

Most Data Scientists will develop Predictive Models as the deliverables of their work.

A Predictive Model is based on determining factors that predict the likelihood that a certain scenario will take place. For example, scientists build predictive models based on factors such as athletes' past stats and weather forecast to predict who is most likely to win the Super Bowl.

In data science, predictive models are primarily used to decide if a set of observations predicts an outcome that can be a label or a value of a measurable quantity. For instance, a decision by a self-driving car whether what is in front of it is an empty road, a car, a person or an object by means of its sensory inputs. This would require a predictive model whose output at any given instant is a label: "road", "car", "person", "object".

On the other hand, our autonomous car may try to predict the arrival time to destination in hours and minutes based on its location, destination distance and traffic conditions. In this case the predictive model produces an outcome -- an estimation of travel time, such as "2 hours" -- that is a quantitative prediction.

In data science lingo, the first model solves a *classification* problem, whereas the second solves a *regression* problem.

Predictive models learn patterns and relationships in the data that happened in the past, with the assumption that these patterns and relations continuous to hold in the future, where we want to make predictions. These patterns and relationships are learned automatically by means of machine learning algorithms. Data scientists select, design and tweak learning algorithms to build predictive models that serve the business needs of the company.

What is an algorithm?

An algorithm is a set of specific steps to be followed in order to achieve a result. Algorithms are used to do complex calculations - such as, find a certain number in a large list of random numbers - and can be then re-used in other applications - for example, in determining the geographic coordinates of a house.

Many times, an algorithm is explained visually with a flow chart:

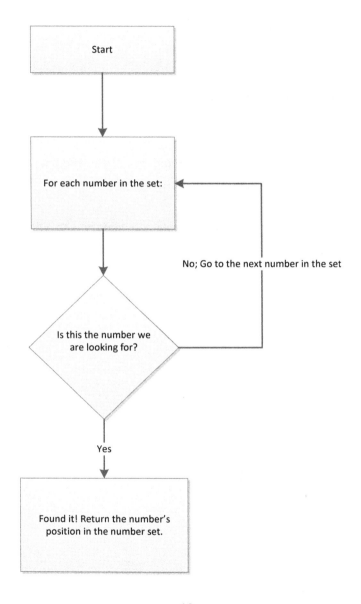

Why use algorithms? Because they can be used as building blocks for our models, and they will simplify our work. If we have the algorithm that always finds a number for us, and it is written in an optimized and efficient way, it will save us lots of time when using it, instead of re-writing the code ourselves every single time.

Algorithms get complicated fast. In data science, the algorithms used are complex searches and decision making, with names such as Random Forest or Linear Regression.

What do I need to become a Data Scientist?

Being a Data Scientist involves a lot of knowledge and formal training. Even for an entry job or internship in the field, you will have to put in a lot of work to achieve the minimum requirements. That being said, this can be accomplished at no cost using free university courses online, and the many free resources available. All you need is passion and a lot of hard work.

At a bare minimum, we recommend that you consider a career in Data Science if you have the following knowledge:

1. Numerical reasoning. Do you like numbers? Are you good at calculating percentages, interest rates, and so forth?
2. Statistics. This is the basis of data science and you need to understand the basic concepts of it.
3. SQL or another query language. You will need to get the data out of databases, and you need to be familiar with the tools you can use for that.
4. R or Python, or another programming language that allows working with large quantities of data.

You can learn and train in each of these areas for free online. Some links are provided in a section below for your reference.

As Easy As Apple Pie?

Any Data Science project uses the scientific method as a basis for development. The scientific method has the following steps (from Wikipedia):

1. Define the question
2. Gather information and resources (observe)
3. Form an explanatory hypothesis
4. Test the hypothesis by performing an experiment and collecting data in a reproducible manner
5. Analyze the data
6. Interpret the data and draw conclusions that serve as a starting point for new hypothesis
7. Publish results
8. Retest

To understand how to think about a Data Science project using the scientific method, imagine you are on a TV mystery cooking show and you are being asked to make an apple pie. You can access a pantry full of ingredients of all kinds, however, you have no recipe! The point of the Data Science project is to figure out how to pick data elements (your ingredients) and combine them using an algorithm (a recipe) to produce a great improvement in a certain outcome you desire (a delicious pie!).

Define the question

The question we want to ask is very important for our project. If we ask the wrong question, such as "How many eggs should I use?", we might be thrown intoa wild goose chase for finding the ideal number of eggs for the dough to be consistent, but we will never get to bake it. The question we should ask is the one that gives you tangible results - in this case, "How can I make an apple pie?"

Gather information and resources - Check your pantry, and prepare your ingredients

The more ingredients you have, the better. If you have several types of apples, sugar and low-carb sweeteners, different kinds of flour and many spices in your pantry, you will increase your chances for a delicious result.

In the end, you need to pick some ingredients out of the entire pantry that you think will play a major role. Since it is an apple pie, I will pick apples, and maybe flour, sugar and eggs for the crust. And how about extras, like cinnamon, lemon, and pecans and caramel sauce?

In order to use the ingredients you picked, you have to prepare them. You need to peel and core the apples, and cut them in thin slices. Make the caramel sauce in a pan. Wash and prepare the pecans. Grind some lemon peel. Crack the eggs in a bowl. Make sure you have measuring tools and baking tools ready.

Form an explanatory hypothesis - Choose a recipe or two

You are not sure how to make an apple pie from scratch, but you can try some basic approaches and see what works. Let's say you decide to try this combination:

Recipe 1.
For the crust, mix together some flour, 2 eggs, and 1 tablespoon of baking soda.
For the filling, toss Granny Smith apple slices with a pinch of cinnamon and sugar.

You are also considering another recipe that you think might work.

Recipe 2.

For the crust, mix together some flour, some butter (melted), and 1 tablespoon of baking soda.
For the filling, toss Red Delicious apple slices with lemon rind, pecans, and sugar.

You put it all together and bake a pie using Recipe 1, however when you taste it you can see there's some room for improvement. The crust is kind of crumbly, and because you chose tart apples, the filling is not sweet enough.

Your second recipe yields a much better-tasting crust, but the apples you chose were too soft and did not hold up well in the pie - now you have a mushy filling with confused pecans sticking out.

You might decide to combine the two recipes - or you might decide Recipe 1 or Recipe 2 perfectly suits your taste and no change is needed. Either way, you found your algorithm that you will follow to bake the pie!

Bake some test pies - Test the hypothesis

Let's say you decided that Recipe 2 has all the major elements that you want in your final pie, and you decide you stick with it.

The next step is to make adjustments to the recipe, until you figure out the exact quantities for the ingredients.

You will need to bake lots of test pies! One with 1 tablespoon with sugar, one with ½ cups of sugar, one with a full cup of sugar.... Until the pie tastes just as sweet as you want it to.

You will do the same adjusting the butter, the apple type and quantity, and so forth. You will have to bake many, many test pies until you get the outcome you want - the best-tasting pie with the right textures and flavors.

Sometimes while testing, a new ingredient might pop up. For example, when you pull your pie out of the oven, you might notice that the butter and the sugar have melted together into sweet caramelized goodness. You were not aware that this could happen, but now, you can use this knowledge to add caramelized sugar to your pie crust - and improve your outcome.

Bake Your Pie - Publish your results

Now that you have all the ingredients and their weight figured out, you will for sure win that cooking show on TV! Then you can even write down your original Recipe and publish it on your Facebook page or cooking blog. You are now guaranteeing that anyone who is using these ingredients and applying your Recipe to them, will most likely have a delicious pie as their successful outcome.

How is the work organized?

A Data Scientist will most likely work on a project. What is a project? It's a group activity that has a beginning and an end, and that produces a specific result.

The Data Scientist will most probably be asked to develop a model, based on the CRISP-DM methodology. CRISP-DM stands for Cross Industry Standard Process for Data Mining.

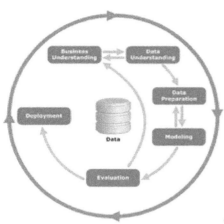

Source: Wikipedia.

CRISP-DM has six major phases that break down the process of data modeling:

1. **Business Understanding**. The most important part of a data science project is understanding the problem we are trying to solve. You need to make sure we develop a project that will add value to our company and/or address a business need. It is particularly easy to get lost in the data and start seeing interesting patterns you want to study forward; but always keep in mind that you first and foremost have to address the business question that started your project.

19

Most of the time, the Project Manager or Product
Owner, along with a Business Analyst, will be
the ones having preliminary discussions with the
business customers. They might create
documents such as a Project Charter to kick-off
the project. You, as a Data Scientist, will be
called into the discussions in order to define the
scope of the project, discuss the business
question and propose ways to address it.

2. **Data understanding**. Also called data
    exploration, in this phase you will start collecting
    all the data you think you will use. You will
    explore it, get familiar with it, and identify any
    issues you might have when using this data for
    your model going forward.

3. **Data Preparation**. This phase allows you to
    finalize your data selection for your model. You
    will pick the databases, tables and attributes you
    want to use. You will come up with rules if data
    is incomplete or has values you cannot use. At
    the end of this phase, you might have an
    Analytical Base Table - a table that contains all

the variables you will need to build a predictive data model.

4. **Modeling**. You will choose a machine learning algorithm, such as linear regression or random forests, that best suits your business problem. You will use a tool to develop and train the model.

5. **Evaluation**. You should evaluate your model when it's ready to deploy, and make sure the business question is answered clearly and correctly. Having a presentation to your stakeholders is probably a good idea at this point, to make sure you are all on the same page and have the same expectations from the model. It is also the time to define and document how you will measure the success of the model by clearly stating your performance metrics.

6. **Deployment**. Once the model is done and returning results, you will need to work with your analyst and your infrastructure team to deploy the model so your business customer can use it in their process (a website, an app, or a report).

Apples to Apples

Data Scientists are hired to create predictive models that answer a certain business question. There is a lot of unknown when they start a new project. They have lots of data to look at (similar with the ingredients in the apple pie) but they do not yet know if and how that data fits together in an algorithm (recipe) that will predict a successful outcome.

Because of the unknown element in a Data Science project, often times they are handled differently than regular software development projects. Your deadlines might be longer, or the methodology used to manage the project might be more fluid (such as Kanban instead of Scrum, if you are working in an Agile environment).

But let's go back our apple pie! First, you want to make sure you understand the rules of the game: what is the goal of the project, what are the limitations, and what is expected of you as the end result. This is part of the Business Understanding in the CRISP-DM methodology.

Check Your Pantry: Identifying Variables

Similar to looking through the pantry to choose ingredients you think might help, Data Scientists do a lot of data explorations to find bits and pieces of data that might help in the model. This is part of the Data Understanding in the CRISP-DM methodology.

Let's discuss a real-life project. Let's assume you work at a small toy store, and the business question you are asked to address is: how can we sell more of the new toy giraffes?

You would need to collect all the data you consider relevant - sales data, customer data, pricing, inventory, anything and everything that might help give you an answer. Of all that data, start identifying data elements that you think could predict a sale (or a failure of a sale) of the giraffe toy:

- Customer Order History - did they buy the giraffe before? Then chances are they will not buy it again.

- Customer Income Level - the giraffe is expensive, and if the customer's income level is low, chances are they will not spend that money.
- Kids' age and gender - if the customer buys regularly toys for baby girls up to 2 years old, they will probably not buy the giraffe which is for 5 year olds.

Prepare Your Ingredients: Clean Your Data

If only all the data in the world would be tamed and beautifully organized and sitting in tiny boxes in perfectly defined matrixes everywhere. How easy it would be to just pick it up and use it when needed!

In reality, your company's data is probably scattered in many databases, varying from legacy to cutting-edge technologies. There could be a data warehouse that stores well-defined, structured data. There could be many applications that collect data and send some of it to the warehouse. Either way, when you are trying to bring this data in to use it in your model, it will have to be organized in a way that makes sense to you.

The data you brought together is almost always not ready to be used for modelling as is. You need to clean and transform it.

Cleaning the data involves getting rid or replacing bad values, such as empty fields that later on might hinder your calculations. Transforming the data means making some values more in tune with your needs for the model. For example, some customers might be missing their first names, or their kids' age. You need to decide if these data elements are important to your model, and if so, what default values can you give them (how can you transform them) when they are not populated with any real data.

This is part of the Data Preparation in the CRISP-DM methodology.

Choose a Recipe or Two: Find Algorithms

It is time to build your model. This is part of the Modeling phase in the CRISP-DM methodology.

You will build your model using a tool - there are several out there, such as IBM's SPSS Modeler. Many companies have built entire platforms to enable data analysis and analytics: IBM, Oracle, SAS, and others. Some of them, such as Revolution Analytics (recently acquired by Microsoft), offers a free community version of their software that you can download and use for your leaning.

Chances are the company where you will find your first job as a Data Scientist already has a specific software platform and a set of tools they use for their data modeling. You will need to learn the new tools but if you already are familiar with one of them it will be much easier. Some of the newest platforms (such as Alteryx) make it easier to create a data model without any code at all by providing a rich user interface where you can visually manipulate objects and data.

Once you have identified the variables you need for your model, and they are nice and clean, it's time to choose your recipe -an algorithm. If all we had as our input data was the order value for customers, and we tried to predict if the customer will be inclined to place an order for the giraffe, we can choose a simple algorithm like a Linear Regression.

Chances are you will have to try several learning algorithms before you settle for one that gives you the best performance.

One of the most used statistical algorithms in Data Science is Random Forest. It uses several data elements as inputs, and it predicts the probability of a successful outcome accurately. If you understand this algorithm, chances are you will be using it to answer many business questions.

Random Forest explained

The term "forest" already implies that this algorithm uses a bunch of trees. Specifically, decision trees that take in some input information and then pop out a yes/no response. A random forest is a collection of many trees, and their answers are combined into a singular, stronger and more accurate answer. There is power in numbers!

Let's say you are looking for a job and you go to LinkedIn where you find a position that really interests you. However there are some pros and also cons to taking the job, so before you apply you want to be sure it's the right thing to do and you will not be wasting your time. It is with a great company, but the location involves a long commute. The salary is good, but the benefits are minimal. Telecommuting is not offered. However they are famous for promoting people once they get in.

Maybe the first person you ask is your mentor: "Do you think this job would be a good fit for me?" Your mentor will come back with a yes/no answer: Yes, because the reputation of the company will really help you advance your career .This was a single decision tree you used.

Now think about sharing your interest in the job with your friends and family. Each of them knows you well but has a slightly different vision of who you are. When you ask the question: "Do you think this job would be a good fit for me?" they will come back with yes/no answers based on their knowledge of your personality and skills. Your girlfriend might suggest that the long commute will mean less time spent going out together. Your Dad might encourage you to follow the good money and take it. Your best friend might think this job will sharpen your current skills and make you gain new ones. And so forth.

You now have a random forest of decision makers. If the large majority of your decision makers answered "Yes", then you will be encouraged to apply for the job, knowing all the arguments that point towards it.

It is not necessary for you to learn or reproduce the inner workings of all algorithms available to explore the data. Most of the algorithms are part of the platform you will be using. However, it helps to understand what they do so you can use it correctly in your model.

While you are exploring the data you have by using different algorithms, it is very possible that you will discover something unexpected. For example, you might find that 70% of customers who bought a giraffe in the past also bought a safari hat. This is very good information that you should immediately share with the store owner, so they can make good use of it - maybe they'll decide to display the giraffes right next to the safari hats.

Bake Some Test Pies: Train Your Model

Once you choose the right algorithm for your project, you need to train your model. This means running the algorithm, tuning the input variables you've defined, until you find the best combination of parameters for each variable that produces the most successful outcome.

To prove that your model is good, you or a business analyst might have to measure the performance of the model. That means they will send an email to a lot of customers advertising a discount on the giraffe, then look and see which customer actually bought the toy, and was it really one of the customers predicted by the model? What the business customers will measure and how will the model be evaluated should be discussed at the beginning of the project, before you design the model. You should then make sure that the value that your model brings is visible and can be shown in performance metrics reports.

This is part of the Evaluation phase in the CRISP-DM methodology.

Bake Your Pie: Deploy Your Model

Now that you know how to make your model predict success, you will have to turn it over to a different team (software engineers and/or systems analysts) that will wrap your model in a webservice or find some other way to embed it into the consumer application. The model itself has no business value until it is actually a part of a business process or application. This is part of the Deployment phase in the CRISP-DM methodology.

For example, let's say we've managed to identify a bunch of variables and a good algorithm that will calculate the probability for each customer to buy our toy giraffe. How do we use this model now in order to increase our sales?

One option could be that we choose the top 20% of customers most likely to buy it, and we send them an email with a special offer for the giraffe. Another option could be that when the customer logs in to our store's website, we know they are highly likely to buy the giraffe so we display it at the top of their search page. How exactly to use your model will be decided by your business customers.

A few pieces of advice for your first job as a Data Scientist:

- Take time to learn and understand your company's data.

- Learn the tools the company uses for developing models.
- Learn from the senior data scientists every day, and ask if one can be your mentor.
- If possible, re-use models that have been already done and verified.

3. HOW TO GET THE JOB?

You see that being a good Data Scientist is not out of reach for someone who is willing to work hard. This book is meant to introduce you to an entry-level position as a Data Scientist in the I.T. world.

There is, of course, much more to learn out there, and you can get a lot of additional information about the field absolutely free! Start by searching the Internet for the terms and concepts I've explained in this booklet.

Start from simple sites like Wikipedia before delving into more complex discussions, Companies like Coursera, Khan Academy, Udacity, edX, Udemy and others offer free or inexpensive courses to sharpen your skills. All it takes is your hard work!

Networking is also a great way to learn about data science and meet with actual Data Scientists who can help and mentor you. Look up Meetups in your local area. Sometimes you can set up informational interviews with people who already do the job, so you can get some real-life details about it.

The Kaggle.com website offers sets of data for rising data scientists, and contest with monetary prizes. It is a great place to learn and develop your first models. After all, your models will predict the future so the possibilities for real-world applications are endless - who will win the Superbowl? Who will be the next President? How tall will be son be when he grows up? You can be very popular with your friends by predicting outcomes, and given enough data and hard work, you should be able to have lots of fun.

Data Science is one area where you can easily create your own projects. Python and R are both free to download and use. Save the code on sites such as GitHub and add the links to your LinkedIn profile, so recruiters can quickly see your work.

You might also want to consider a strong social media presence. A blog or online posts about your projects and your interest in Data Science will convince employers of your enthusiasm and ability.

Finding and Applying for Jobs

Technical jobs are everywhere, and Data Scientists are currently in very high demand. If you like a particular company (maybe because it is close to your home), check out its website and sign up to receive its job alerts.

Set up a profile on LinkedIn. It's free, and it will put you in touch with other professionals, as well as headhunters/recruiters. Update your resume and post it for free on websites like Indeed.com, Monster.com and Dice.com. If you are worried that your resume is not good enough, hire a career services firm to redo it for you. Oftentimes these companies offer deals through Groupon or Living Social, and you will get a good discount.

Do not be shy. Ask your friends and family if they know of any open positions. When my husband was laid off from his job, we asked everyone we knew and the person that ultimately led to a new job was another mom from my son's basketball team. You never know where useful information will come from,

When applying for jobs, update your resume slightly to accentuate the requirements for each specific job. Do not just blindly send the same resume for every job.

A cover letter is sometimes recommended along with the resume. There are numerous samples online that you can use to create a simple letter, but don't forget to customize it every time you send it. Highlight things that are close to the job description, and send it directly to a specific person if possible.

Be honest about being a beginner in the field, but let them know of all the work you've done by yourself to prepare, and your passion for data science.

Whatever you do, do not lie in your resume or cover letter. Most companies run background checks, and they will catch you and fire you immediately.

Be careful about scams. There are many folks online who pretend to be recruiters, but they are not legitimate. Here are some warning signs:

- They ask you for money. Anyone who does this is not a real recruiter.
- They ask for your resume, but they don't have a specific position to fill.
- They ask for your bank account number, social security number, or any other private information.

Interviewing for the Job

Interviews in the new I.T. industry usually have three parts. First, you will get a phone call from a recruiter-- either someone in the company's HR department or a paid headhunter.

This first phone interview is called 'screening'. It means your resume caught someone's attention who'd like to find out more about you. This interview is all about first impressions. Be prepared to discuss your background, and answer any questions about your resume and cover letter. Be short and clear in your answers, and do not give away too much information if it's not needed.

If all goes well, you'll get a second interview. This means you are one of the few candidates selected, so you made it out of the first round. The second interview is usually with the hiring manager directly, sometimes along with other folks on the team. This is your chance to shine.

The second interview can be over the phone or in person. If it's over the phone, prepare for at least a 30-minute (if not longer) discussion. So find a quiet place where you can use a speaker phone to make sure you don't miss anything.

If the interview is in person, dress appropriately; that is, wear a dark dress or suit with a solid-color shirt and minimal jewelry. Do some research on the traffic conditions expected during the time you'll be travelling to your interview, and determine whether and where there is available parking. Make sure you know where to go and how to get there. If you have time, do a dry run to see how long it takes you to get to the location.

The second interview is all about your job skills. You might get an actual technical test, where you are asked to analyze data or to write SQL or R code. The best advice I can give you is to discuss projects you have worked on. Give details about the project scope, methodology, and impact. It could be a personal project or a volunteer project; it doesn't matter, as long as you can enthusiastically discuss it and your contribution to it.

I also recommend strongly that you carry some samples of your work. A presentation or a collection of graphs from a few projects you worked on, that you can easily bring up as you discuss the project.

Sometimes there are also behavioral questions. Look these up on the Internet for some examples. Practice responding to some of these at home so you can have prepared answers for questions such as, "What was your greatest accomplishment and how did you achieve it?" or "Tell me about a time you faced an obstacle at work and how you overcame it." Discuss actual details from the projects you worked on, and you will prove your experience and enthusiasm.

Be sure to look people in the eye as you speak. Appear confident and knowledgeable. Do not forget to ask questions: This is your best chance to find out details about the job, the company, and what the problems are. (Everyone has problems!) One question I like to ask is, "Can you tell me what some of the main challenges are in this job?" Jot down some notes for later reference.

If all goes well, you might get a third interview, although this is usually for more senior positions. This interview is usually with the hiring manager's superiors, so you need to step up your game.

This interview is not about your job skills. This one is to determine what value you can bring to the company and whether you can think strategically enough to be a good asset. You have to expect behavioral questions in this interview, Think of scenarios where you helped save money, saved resources, sped up delivery time, or successfully dealt with a conflict in your team. These are the kinds of leadership behaviors that will be measured.

My best trick for this interview is to walk in with a lot of confidence, as if you already have the job. You need to speak of your strategic approach to the job and how you will improve the bottom line. By now you know some things about the organization's problems (since you asked them at the second interview), so you should have some suggestions about how you can alleviate its pain points by doing your job.

No one is calling! What Am I Doing Wrong?

If you don't get any calls after posting your resume, then your resume is weak. Get a resume writing professional to fix it.

If you get several first interviews but they never call for a second, you are saying or doing something wrong. Ask a friend to listen to you when you talk to a recruiter and see what you are saying to turn them off.

If you get a bunch of second interviews but no thirds and no offers, then you come off wrong in the face-to-face situations. Again, check with a friend and practice a mock interview at home to get some constructive feedback.

It takes months for even the best, most experienced I.T. people to find a new job. Do not be discouraged if it takes a long time. Use the time to create even more projects that you can brag about. Finding a job is like finding someone to date. Sometimes they like you, but you don't like them; sometimes you love them but the feeling's not mutual. And no one tells the whole truth on the first date. The match simply has to work for both sides to ensure it will be a good, productive, satisfactory job fit.

Final Note

Check out our website for more books in this series and for ideas, articles and more suggestions. You can also contact the authors and read about others' experiences breaking into the new I.T.

The new Information Technology is no longer for geeks, math fanatics, or video game-obsessed nerds. The truth is, I.T. has now taken over everything in our lives and in doing so, it has created new jobs requiring all kinds of skills and abilities.

You do not need a computer science degree to get an entry-level job in I.T. that pays well and offers benefits. You do not need any expensive certifications or courses. You need passion, ambition, this book to help you get started, lots of hard work and a bit of luck.

Here's to your success!

--- The End ---

www.ingramcontent.com/pod-product-compliance
Lightning Source LLC
Chambersburg PA
CBHW051217050326
40689CB00008B/1343